SUMMARY
of Jim Collin's
GOOD TO GREAT

Why Some Companies Make the Leap and Others Don't

by SUMOREADS

TABLE OF CONTENTS

EXECUTIVE SUMMARY

Jim Collin's *Good to Great* examines companies that have not only endured over time, but who managed the transition from being good companies to becoming outstanding performers. The eleven companies found to have taken this leap managed to outperform the stock market 6.9 times over fifteen years. The author set out to understand what distinguished great organizations from a carefully selected group of companies who did not make the grade.

The research team came up with some unexpected outcomes. At the time of the transition from Good to Great all eleven companies were being led by Level 5 Leaders. These people showed a unique combination of humility and professional will. They were prepared to do anything necessary for the benefit of the organization.

The Level 5 Leaders started out, not by plotting the direction of the company, but by ensuring that they had all the right people in the right positions. Then they confronted the brutal facts of their organization, using this knowledge to ensure that they chose the right direction for the firm. Knowing what the organization should be doing—and equally importantly what it should not be doing—they stuck stubbornly to the plan even when they were in dire circumstances. The culture of discipline within the organization ensured that the path to excellence would eventually be met. Patience, endurance and discipline, doggedly sticking only to what the company did best, resulted in outstanding results.

This investigation of what distinguished the great from the mediocre is an excellent study of what is needed to build great organizations.

CHAPTER SUMMARIES

CHAPTER 1: GOOD IS THE ENEMY OF GREAT

Why do so many organizations fail to move from good companies to great companies? Based on a tight set of criteria, a research team identified eleven companies that had stood the test of time, and that had over the past fifteen years made superior returns.

The team identified seven essential attributes, which these companies uniquely shared. They were:

• Level 5 Leadership

• The right people in the right positions

• The ability to confront the realities of the business

• The ability to be the best in the industry

• A culture of discipline throughout the organization

• The ability to choose the technologies which would drive change

• The ability to manage change organically rather than through revolutionary methods

"Greatness is not a function of circumstance. Greatness, it turns out, is largely a matter of conscious choice, and discipline."

CHAPTER 2: LEVEL 5 LEADERSHIP

Every one of the Good to Great companies had at their head a Level 5 Leader at the time of transition. These leaders exhibit a unique combination of personal humility and professional will. They put the success of their organization ahead of personal success. They are driven to do whatever it takes, regardless of the personal cost, to ensure that their organization reaches the top of its game. These leaders ensured that the organization would last well beyond their own departure.

The leaders of the comparison companies tended to be more concerned about their own reputation and wealth accumulation. Over 75 percent of these leaders failed to build the foundations required to ensure sustainable success. In more than 66 percent of the comparison companies, personal egos contributed to the organization failing to flourish.

"The good-to-great leaders never wanted to become larger-than-life heroes. They never aspired to be put on a pedestal or become unreachable icons. They were seemingly ordinary people quietly producing extraordinary results"

CHAPTER 3: FIRST WHO…THEN WHAT

Determining the strategy of the organization was not the first concern of Level 5 Leaders. Their first concern was to ensure that they had the right people in the right positions. They employed people with the right set of values who would help to take the company to a successful future. In addition, employees within the organization were redeployed to more suitable positions, and those who could not fit in were removed. Only once the right people were in place did the leaders decide on the direction that the company would take. These leaders understood that with committed, self-motivated and disciplined people in place, it would be easier to make changes in strategic direction.

"Those who build great companies understand that the ultimate throttle on growth for any great company is not markets, or technology, or competition, or products. It is one thing above all others: the ability to get and keep enough of the right people."

CHAPTER 4: CONFRONT THE BRUTAL FACTS (YET NEVER LOSE FAITH)

Without fail the Good to Great breakthrough came about as a result of good decisions being well implemented. These companies had faced the brutal facts, and used them as a framework for developing all their decisions. Comparison companies failed to do this. In many comparison companies the executives were too afraid of the leader to convince him of the realities. This inevitably led to mediocre company performance. Leadership is not just about vision. It is also about creating an environment where employees can be heard.

Many of the comparison companies, when faced with unpleasant realities, were overwhelmed and were prepared to concede defeat. Good to Great companies did not give up when faced with the ugly truth; instead they were invigorated and energized, and more determined to fight to be the best in their industry. Whilst they understood the facts, they had unfaltering faith in their ability to win in the end.

CHAPTER 5: THE HEDGEHOG CONCEPT (SIMPLICITY WITHIN THE THREE CIRCLES)

An ancient Greek parable teaches that "The fox knows many things, but the hedgehog knows one big thing." In the world of business there are companies who see the complexities of the world and attempt to pursue many different directions. These are the foxes. Then there are those who seek to simplify the complexities into simple ideas. These are hedgehogs. The Good to Great companies all sought to simplify the complexities of the environments in which they operated, reducing it to a simple Hedgehog Concept. The comparative companies failed to do this.

Developing a Hedgehog Concept is not about setting objectives; it is about knowing what the organization does best. Good to Great companies instinctively knew what they did best and never got side tracked into doing anything else. They understood what they had to do to be the best in the industry. They knew exactly what direction they would take because they understood the realities. The comparative companies never understood the realities, setting strategies without the required knowledge.

CHAPTER 6: A CULTURE OF DISCIPLINE

Undisciplined people need careful management. Organizations develop bureaucratic systems to manage employees, who require careful management. Bureaucratic management frustrates those employees who have an entrepreneurial spirit, those who are disciplined and self-motivated. In this way bureaucracy kills entrepreneurial spirit.

In creating a culture of discipline, bureaucracy can be dispensed with. Level 5 leaders built sustainable cultures of discipline. In the comparative companies, the leader was the driving force behind the discipline in the organization. This approach to discipline cannot endure beyond the leader.

Disciplined action must be built upon the understanding of the reality. Good to Great companies remained fully committed to the Hedgehog Concept. Everything they did had to fit with the concept. They took deliberate actions to eliminate anything that did not support the Hedgehog Concept. It was an all or nothing approach demonstrating the unwavering commitment to that which they did best. Every comparison company either lacked the discipline to understand the concept, or did not have the discipline to stay consistently true to it.

"When you have disciplined thought, you don't need bureaucracy. When you have disciplined action, you don't need excessive controls."

CHAPTER 7: TECHNOLOGY ACCELERATORS

Technology does not create growth, but when the correct technology is selected it can accelerate growth. Good to Great companies understood that only those technologies that supported the Hedgehog Concept were relevant and should be considered. They were disciplined in their approach to technology, avoiding technologies that did not support this concept. They embraced the technologies that did, and were often pioneers in the application of these technologies. Comparative companies frequently lurched into new technologies, without too much thought, motivated by fear of being left behind.

Research found that technology neither caused the decline of organizations nor was it the cause of greatness.

CHAPTER 8: THE FLYWHEEL AND THE DOOM LOOP

The transition in Good to Great companies did not happen in an instant. It was the result of an accumulation actions; the development of a process that finally added up to outstanding results. There was no single event that suddenly led to a breakthrough. In Good to Great companies the transformation happened through a slow and deliberate process, an accumulation of actions that resulted in the breakthrough moment. Even serious circumstances, such as financial loss, could not divert Good to Great companies from their chosen course of action. These companies remained patient and disciplined. The comparative companies tended to succumb to short-term pressures.

The Good to Great companies took consistent actions within the framework of the Hedgehog Concept, accumulating positive results, which further energised the stakeholders, building the momentum that finally led to the transition. This is the flywheel effect.

CHAPTER 9: FROM GOOD TO GREAT TO BUILT TO LAST

Enduring great companies have core ideologies. They do not exist simply to make money. Every great company must have core values. There is no specific set of values that will work, but the values must be built into an organization, and must be preserved over time. Strategies and practices should be adapted to keep abreast of the changing business environment, but the core purpose of the organization must be preserved.

The eleven companies that made the transition from good to great demonstrated behaviors which can be applied to any organizational structure. Methodically applying these concepts and dropping all other principles makes life simpler and results in outstanding returns. Failure to carry out the concepts practiced by the great companies will quickly lead to backsliding.

KEY TAKEAWAYS

Key Takeaway: Every Great Company Had a Level 5 Leader

The Chief Executive Officers of all eleven outstanding companies were Level 5 Leaders. Level 5 Leaders are driven to produce outstanding results, and will fearlessly do whatever is required to ensure the success of the organization. These leaders attribute their success to others, declining to take the credit. They do, however, accept full responsibility for failures. They demand the highest standards of performance. They are generally modest people, shunning publicity and needing no public approval. Their ambitions are for the success of the business rather than for themselves. Level 5 Leaders will always set the organization up for a successful future, which goes beyond their tenure.

Leaders of the comparison companies tended to apportion blame for failures, but accepted the praise for successes. They failed to set the organization up for sustainable success.

Key Takeaway: The Right People Can Help Steer the Organization in the Right Direction

Leaders of Good to Great companies know that the people they employ are of greater importance than the strategy or vision. "People are not your most important asset. The right people are" The right people are easy to manage, as they are self-motivated, disciplined and committed. Bureaucratic systems become necessary when the organization employs undisciplined people. This, in turn, kills the entrepreneurial spirit in the organization.

Personal attributes such as work ethic and values are more important than skills and knowledge, which can be taught.

Key Takeaway: There Is No Correlation Between Executive Reward and Great Performance, But Rewards Are Necessary to Attract the Right People

The research team found no correlation between executive reward and the company's transition from good to great. Compensation does not provide motivation for a Level 5 Leader, as he is already hardwired to do the best that he can to ensure that the organization produces outstanding results over an extended period.

Compensation should however, be used to ensure that the right leader is attracted to the organization in the first place. This is true through every level of the organization. Compensation attracts the right people to the organization. The right people are self-motivated.

Key Takeaway: Create an Environment Where People Can Be Heard

Leadership is not only about vision. It is also about creating an environment where employees can be heard. This environment can be created by asking questions with a view to understanding, engaging in discussions with all parties, talking without debating, and by clinically analyzing mistakes without allotting blame.

In the Good to Great companies, there were vigorous discussions before conclusions were reached. In some of the comparative companies, the employees all the way up to executive management were too in awe of the leader to bring information to his attention.

Key Takeaway: Create Red Flags

There was an abundance of information available at both the Good to Great and the comparative companies, but it was not always used. "Red flags" should be used to ensure that the necessary information is highlighted and cannot be ignored.

Key Takeaway: Great Companies Do Not Give Up When Faced with the Realities

Good to Great companies were not overwhelmed when faced with the facts, no matter how brutal the truth. Instead, they were newly committed and energized to remain the best in their industry. Whilst they understood the facts, they never lost faith in their ability to win in the end. The comparative companies, when they understood the realities, were not prepared for the fight, choosing rather to surrender.

Key Takeaway: Great Companies Were Adept at Understanding What They Should Be Doing and, Equally Importantly, What They Should Not Be Doing

The Good to Great companies understood what they did best. They also knew what they could not do well. They understood the source of their cash flows and profits. These facts, along with a passion for what they did, formed the basis of their Hedgehog Concept. They understood that if you could not be the best in the world at what you did, you should not be doing it—even if that was the core competency of the business. They knew what they did best, and they never allowed themselves to become side tracked into doing anything else even when the going got tough.

The big difference between the comparative companies and the Good to Great companies was that the Good to Great companies, in understanding the realities, knew exactly what direction they would take. The comparative companies set strategies in ignorance of the realities.

Key Takeaway: Great Companies Understand Their Economic Drivers

Every one of Good to Great companies understood the key economic drivers of their business and built a system to support these. The key driver to success was in understanding the profit per unit. The foundation of the organization's success would determine which unit would be chosen. The unit (or denominator) had to be determined by understanding which element of the business would have the biggest and most enduring impact in driving the long-term success of the organization.

The Good to Great organizations were all profoundly aware of what their economic denominator was. The comparison companies frequently were not.

Key Takeaway: Good to Great Companies Were Rigorous in the Employment of the Right People

Although Good to Great companies were rigorous in the application of their employment, redeployment, and release of personnel, they were not ruthless. They were far less likely to embark on restructuring or layoff procedures than the comparison companies

They applied a set of guidelines:

They did not hire if there was any doubt about the suitability of the candidate. They believed that company growth is determined by the company's ability to hire and retain enough of the right employees, and not by the market, the competitors or any other external factor.

If the removal of an employee became necessary, immediate action was taken, as they realized that poor performers cause frustration amongst the employees who they wished to retain.

The best opportunities and not the biggest problems were offered to the best employees.

Key Takeaway: Executive Teams in Great Companies Debate Amongst Themselves and Then Unify Around the Decision

In Good to Great companies, the executive teams tended to emulate the Level 5 Leaders. They were able to stand their ground, rigorously debating issues amongst themselves, and then unifying around the final conclusion.

Key Takeaway: Great Companies Build a Culture of Discipline

Level 5 leaders build sustainable cultures of discipline. Disciplined action must be built upon the understanding of reality. Good to Great companies remained fully committed to the Hedgehog Concept. Everything they did had to fit. If it didn't, they did not do it. Every comparison company either lacked the discipline to understand the concept, or the discipline to stay consistently true to it. The Good to Great companies took deliberate actions to eliminate anything that did not support the Hedgehog Concept.

Great companies start with disciplined people. Disciplined thought is required to face reality and find the Hedgehog Concept. From this point the company must move to disciplined action.

Key Takeaway: Manage the System, Not the People

A cohesive system must be built within the disciplined framework of the Hedgehog Concept. Constraints must be built into the system and people must be given freedom and responsibility to operate within this framework. When an organization has self-disciplined, committed employees, the system can be managed rather than the employees.

Consistency and coherence is key. Each element of a system must integrate with every other element, creating a coherent whole. The consistent application of a coherent system will result in sustained success

Key Takeaway: Change is a Process and Not An Occurrence

In Good to Great companies, it was not necessary to drive change, or to set big goals, because the leader had already created an environment in which all employees embraced change. Presenting small gains to the stakeholders created the required momentum to keep the change going. Within the framework of the Hedgehog Concept, the company took consistent actions, which cumulatively led to transition.

The comparative companies tended to launch new strategies and improvement programs, seeking to create change quickly, too impatient to follow the slow change process. These companies failed to gain momentum and fell into the Doom Loop. The Doom Loop starts when disappointing results force a reaction. Without gaining an understanding of the realities, these companies embarked on new programs of change. These were doomed to failure, as the leaders did not have the patience to allow the changes to gain momentum.

Key Takeaway: Acquisitions and Mergers Played No Role in the Transition of the Good to Great Companies

Good to Great companies did not make acquisitions until after the development of their Hedgehog Concept. They also waited until change management had gained some momentum. The result was that the acquisition process was consistently successful. The comparative companies attempted to create breakthrough occurrences through acquisitions. They failed every time.

Key Takeaway: Technology Does Not Create Growth, But it Can Be an Accelerator

As with all other aspects of the business, technology should be chosen only if it supports the Hedgehog Concept. Good to Great companies took a disciplined approach to technology ensuring that it fitted in with the concept. If it did, they vigorously pursued the application of the technology. The comparison companies, afraid of being left behind, tended to pursue new technologies without understanding the realities.

Key Takeaway: Companies Built to Last Must Preserve Their Key Values and Core Purpose

The four key ideas from "Built to Last" were reinforced with the research into Good to Great.

* The business must built to survive

* The organization should have more than a single purpose

• Generations of employees will be guided and inspired by the core values and the core purpose of the business—embrace these

• Whilst preserving core values and core purpose, strategies and practices must be adapted to deal with changes in the environment

EDITORIAL REVIEW

Good to Great by Jim Collins is a well documented and interesting discussion of the five-year investigation into whether companies could make the leap from good to great and if so, how. As the author of *Built to Last*, Collins became curious about what it would take for an organization, which was good but not outstanding, to take the leap from good to great.

To investigate the question, he set up a research team and then embarked on a five-year study of the subject. The team selected companies which had shown cumulative growth at or below the market growth rate for fifteen years, and which had subsequently shown returns of at least three times the market rate for the next fifteen years. The growth had to be independent of industry growth. There were just eleven companies which met the criteria. These companies had made an astonishing cumulative 6.9 times the average return on the stock market over fifteen years.

The initial research had proven that companies could take the leap from Good to Great. The research team now needed to understand what distinguished these companies from a set of carefully chosen comparison companies that did not take the leap. They chose to build evidence from the ground up, rather than attempting to prove or disprove theories. They used qualitative, quantitative and empirical evidence, delving through articles and interviewing employees and leaders of the Good to Great and comparative companies.

The first astonishing find was that the Good to Great companies were all under the leadership of extraordinary people at the time of transition. These individuals "Level 5 Leaders" all possessed a combination of personal humility and professional will. All were driven to do whatever it took to make the organization successful even at great personal sacrifice. The second chapter of the book is dedicated to examining the personal attributes of the Level 5 Leaders, and the rest of the book examines what these leaders did to launch the organization into enduring success.

The research team found the leaders of the Good to Great companies surrounded themselves with disciplined and motivated employees, before they had even decided which route the company would take. They were valiant enough to face the brutal truth about their business. Armed with an understanding of the truth, they developed plans to turn what they did best and were passionate about into a business which provided outstanding returns and which would thrive for generations.

The change that took place in the Good to Great companies was not spontaneous or revolutionary. It was an accumulation of actions which built up to the final breakthrough. It took discipline and patience. It was a deliberate process. The leaders never allowed the organization to be side tracked from the original carefully established goals, no matter how attractive the other opportunities or how dire the circumstances. The right people in the right positions, the hedgehog concept and the culture of discipline all guided by a Level 5 Leader are what allowed these companies to transition from Good to Great.

This is an inspiring book, well written in every day language. It is full of interesting stories and anecdotes of great and not so great leaders and companies. It is imminently readable and the research is convincing.

ABOUT THE AUTHOR

Jim Collins is the co-author of six books, which have sold more than ten million copies. *Good to Great* is a number one best seller, and followed on the heels of *Built to Last*, also a best seller. These books are a culmination of twenty-five of studying best practice in business

Jim Collins started his career at the Stanford Graduate School of Business, where he was a teacher. In 1992, he received the Distinguished Teaching Award. He started a management laboratory in 1995, where he conducts his research, engaging in discussion with senior management teams and Chief Executive Officers.

He has a bachelor's degree in mathematical sciences and an MBA from Stanford.

THE END

If you enjoyed this summary, please leave an honest review on Amazon.com…it'd mean a lot to us.

If you haven't already, we encourage you to purchase a copy of the original book.

Made in United States
North Haven, CT
24 May 2023